Daily Writing Prompts To Spur Creativity

365 Writing Prompts To Get You Started

EJ Divitt

Table of Contents

Foreword 3

1-50 4

51-100 14

101 to 150 24

151-200 34

201-250 43

251-300 54

301-365 64

Bonus 74

More From EJ Divitt 76

The following prompts are intended to give you a jumping off point to spur your creativity. You can do one a day for a year or go through and pick and choose as you please. Try to write at least 300 words for every one. It is not that many words really; it is about twice the length of this foreword.

If one of the prompts gives you a different idea, feel free to write that instead. These are intended to spark ideas and not to lock you in. You can write a poem, a short story, a paragraph or a scene; whatever works for you.

Some are written as "you"; feel free to change it to a fictional character or a fictional version of yourself. There are no rules; just write.

Remember creative writing is like a muscle; the more you use it, the stronger it will be. Happy writing.

1. Write a scene between a young man and his sentient car after he decides to take a cab out on his date.

2. A burnt piece of toast ruined their marriage.

3. Your character develops the ability to shift into a chicken. Unfortunately, he can't control it.

4. Write a scene where each sentence starts with the next letter of the alphabet. For example, "A good time was not had by all. Before the end of the party at least one person would be

hurt. Charles knew it was his own fault." Etc

5. Write a scene that incorporates a fruit, an animal and a public restroom.

6. Death knocks on your door and says, "We need to talk."

7. Zombies come out to society and fight for equal rights.

8. You come home and find your spouse in bed with a pigeon, a bowl of spaghetti and your favorite shirt. Describe the conversation.

9. Write a scene that

includes a mouse, a bulldozer and a tea cup.

10. Pick up the closest book and open it to a random page. Pick one sentence and make that the first sentence in your story.

11. You are a guy preparing to propose to your girlfriend. Write about how you would do it.

12. Write a scene or story that includes a broken cup, a clown and a court house.

13. You find a red hair in your bed when you are a blond.

14. You have been hired to write a magazine ad about

deodorant. Write the ad copy.

15. Write a reunion between two lovers who have been apart for several months.

16. A tea cup is sitting in the middle of your driveway. How did it get there?

17. Pretend you are starting your new job as a brain surgeon. What is the first thing you need to do?

18. You are an acrobat. Write your resume.

19. Write a letter of reference for the hero or heroine of your favorite book.

20. Write a scene that ends with, "So if it wasn't for the goat, I would never have gotten married."

21. Write about what you are wearing right now.

22. "I knew the story would be terrible as soon as I read it was a dark and stormy night." What is the next sentence?

23. Write a scene from the point of few of a new ghost.

24. Write a scene from the point of view of your pet. If you do not have one, make one up.

25. Write a scene between two

horses.

26. Write about the worst thing that ever happened to you.

27. Write about your favorite childhood toy.

28. Describe the perfect vegetable garden.

29. Write a scene about a vampire that faints at the sight of blood.

30. Write about a werewolf who hates to hunt.

31. You are startled awake at night by the a loud crash. What happens next?

32. You are sitting next to

your best friend. They suddenly kiss you. What happens next?

33. Write a letter to God.

34. Write a letter to Santa Claus.

35. You just got a job as the new tooth fairy. Write about your first night on the job.

36. If you could have any one person fired, who would it be? Why? How?

37. Under the Christmas tree, your character finds a box. Inside is their heart's desire. What is it?

38. How many writers does it

take to screw in a light bulb? Why?

39. Your aunt gives you a tiger for your birthday.

40. Write about the perfect kiss.

41. Write about a camping trip where everything goes wrong.

42. Write a goodbye letter to yourself.

43. Write a conversation between a shoe and a rock.

44. Describe the scene outside the closest window.

45. The local deli is naming a sandwich after you. Describe the

sandwich.

46. Your little sister has shaved one side of your beard while you were sleeping. What do you do?

47. How many ways can you think of to say something is blue?

48. Write a scene from the point of view of a box of facial tissues.

49. You are given five minutes to interview your idol. What questions would you ask? What would they answer?

50. You wake up as an animated character. Write would

happens next. Where are you? What happened to you?

51. You wake up one day and find that you have completely lost the ability to speak English.

52. You are lying peacefully in your grave when someone walks over it.

53. Explain the color green to a blind person.

54. You have the ability to levitate. What would you do with it?

55. An eagle flies down and snatches you up. What happens next? Where do you go?

56. You wake up one morning and find you are nine months

pregnant.

57. Your house is surrounded by the National Guard. Why?

58. What lives on the dark side of the moon?

59. Describe a creature that can only breathe coal dust.

60. You are a reality television star. Cameras are following you everywhere you go. What do you do?

61. You are being given a Nobel Prize. What is it for?

62. Your condo association is trying to make you get rid of your pet lion. Why does the lion need

to go? What will you do about it?

63. Your new nickname is Grey. Why?

64. Your two year old asks why is the sky blue? Make up an answer.

65. The goddess of all creation brings you something to guard. What is it? What are you protecting it from?

66. You are introduced to God. He or She tells you to call them by their first name. What is it? Who gave it to them?

67. You are awarded a Medal of Honor. Describe how you earned

it.

68. Your great grandfather's spirit comes to visit you. What do you do? What do you talk about?

69. You are on trial for being too cute.

70. Your daughter returns after an estrangement. What do you do? What caused the gap?

71. You are being taken away into witness protection. What did you see?

72. You are forced to leave your home forever. You may only bring ten items. What are they?

73. A strange meteorite

crashes into your yard and gives you a super power. What super power would you have?

74. What is the weakness of your superpower? Aka what is your kryptonite?

75. What musical instrument do you wish you could play? Why?

76. Your arch enemy is revealed to you at last. Who is it and why?

77. You are president for one day. What do you do?

78. Write an argument between the sun and the moon.

79. A dove, a pig and a sparrow walk into a bar. Describe

the scene.

80. You find out that you are about to die. What do you do with your last day? Your last week? Your last six months?

81. An angel comes to visit you and tells you that only you can save the world. What is your special skill?

82. Describe a day lived backwards.

83. Describe the space between words.

84. Have your character tell their lover that they have found someone else.

85. Explain to a deaf person what your favorite song sounds like.

86. Write a description of the sounds of the room you are in right now.

87. Write the paragraph after this sentence. "I need to get back to the island."

88. You are granted one wish but you can not wish for more wishes. What do you do with it?

89. You are being turned into an animal for your own protection. What animal do you choose? Why?

90. Write a scene in which

you have to explain to a child where babies come from.

91. Your protagonist has a harmless but annoying quirk. They can not stop hopping. Write a scene in which they try to explain this at a job interview.

92. You wake up in bed covered in some one else's blood. Describe what happens.

93. Describe someone seeing snow for the first time.

94. Write a scene in which your father reveals to you that he is an alien.

95. Write a love letter to

your favorite piece of furniture.

96. Write a scene in which you explain to your five year old that there is no Santa Claus.

97. You are standing at the counter drinking your coffee when you suddenly shrink to the size of a spoon.

98. Write a synopsis of your favorite book. Now add either a vampire, a werewolf, a gorilla or an astronaut.

99. Decide who would win in a battle of caveman vs astronaut. Write the final battle.

100. A doctor, a priest, and

a stripper are having dinner together. What do they talk about?

101. What if we are just part of someone else's dream? What would you do?

102. You wake up one morning and the sky has turned orange. What happens next?

103. Write a piece of hate mail to your table.

104. Write a scene about today's Google.com logo.

105. Write a scene from the point of view of an insect.

106. Write a dialog between two flowers in a garden.

107. Write a dialog between two fairy tale characters meeting

for the first time.

108. Write a list of your favorite things. Do not just put the names. Pick at least one and write exactly why they are your favorite things. What makes them good? What would make it better?

109. Describe your favorite thing to someone who has never seen it before.

110. Write a scene between two children who have both just been adopted by the same couple.

111. Write a scene in which you have to confess something to your parents.

112. Write a love scene from the opposite point of view. For example, if you are male, write as a female. If you are straight, write it as though you were gay.

113. Describe the room you are sitting in right now with as much detail as possible. Really pay attention to the shades of color and detail.

114. "Yesterday I killed an ogre." Write the rest of the scene.

115. "Today I told (her/him) that I did not love them anymore." Finish the rest.

116. Start a dialog with the phrase. "Kill me now."

117. Write about the sunset without using the words yellow, red or blue.

118. You are going to be turned into a type of dessert. What kind? Describe it and say why it would most represent you.

119. Your office has dress like a clown day. What do you wear? Describe your outfit or your day.

120. You are picked to sit on the jury of a well known mobster. Describe the court case.

121. Write about your dream home.

122. Write a list of all of your worst characteristics. Now try to find the positive spin on them.

123. Write a commercial for the shoes you are wearing right now.

124. Pick up any book. Turn to page 103. Pick the first nouns in the first two sentences. Write a scene that includes them.

125. Write a story about a dance.

126. Pick your favorite

species or villain from science fiction. Write a scene where you come face to face with them.

127. Pick a news headline from the last couple of days and write the story just from looking at the headline.

128. Add a monster to that news story such as a zombie or werewolf.

129. Write a scene from the point of view of an uninvolved third party.

130. Get up and walk around your desk three times clockwise and three times counterclockwise.

Sit down and right what you were thinking about as you did it.

131. You are forced to give up your favorite drink or die. Write the scene.

132. Write a scene for a children's story about a lion who has to give up his mane.

133. Now write the same scene as though it were a news story.

134. You are suddenly struck mute. What do you do?

135. You develop the ability to communicate with birds. Write the scene where you first use this ability.

136. You awaken in chains and are told you have been sold into slavery. What is the first thing you do?

137. Write a scene from the point of view of someone who just woke up with a fin.

138. Now write the scene from the point of view of their one night stand who just woke up to discover the fin.

139. What is the ideal life for an avocado? Describe it from the point of view of the avocado.

140. Write a paragraph that starts with, "I watched in horror

as the can headed straight for his head."

141. You walk in on your married boss with a stripper and a table full of drugs.

142. Describe your favorite meal in detail.

143. Pick an age and write a scene where you travel back in time to give advice to your younger self.

144. Ask your favorite celebrity to marry you.

145. You are given a free billboard for a day. Write the text for it.

146. Write about your favorite scene in your favorite movie.

147. You are given the ability to shape shift into any animal. What do you pick and why?

148. What is your first day as the shape shifter?

149. How do you break the news to your family?

150. Elephants turn carnivorous.

151. Horses all turn into unicorns.

152. Write a reunion between two former lovers who parted on bad terms.

153. You have to choose to give up one appendage. What do you give up? How do you adjust to life without it?

154. Your older sister suddenly develops psychic powers. What power does she get? Write the scene where she realizes that she has a new power.

155. Write the scene where your sister attacks you with her

new found power.

156. Your house magically flips upside down. Describe trying to navigate through it.

157. Write a scene where you tell your children that you are really a tree.

158. Write a scene where you find out that your father was a spy.

159. Your mother is a double agent. How do you find out?

160. You meet an online date and discover that it is your own mother or father.

161. Your death timer starts

counting down. How long until you die? What do you do with the time?

162. How do you die?

163. Turn on the TV. Whatever the first sentence you hear, write a scene that starts with that sentence.

164. Write a scene that ends with that sentence.

165. A dating site tells you that your perfect match is the exact opposite of what you want.

166. Write a dating website description for a fallen angel.

167. Write one for a mermaid or merman.

168. Someone offers you ten billion dollars but you have to become Batman.

169. You have to leave your house and never come back but you can live anywhere in the world with out worrying about money. Where do you go?

170. Look around where you are or out your window. Make up a story about the first person you see. Who are they? What do they do? Why are they there?

171. Our overlords, the octopuses, have assigned you to write a speech explaining why we

should submit to their benevolent rule.

172. Write a sad childhood memory.

173. You are a woman saying no to a proposal. Write about how it would go.

174. You have a mirror that will show you anyone in the world.

175. God moves in next door. What do you do?

176. You have a chance to go back to being a baby. Write the scene where you accept or decline.

177. Write your day from the point of view of baby you.

178. You wake up and find out you have grown an extra leg overnight.

179. You develop a rare genetic disease that causes you to shrink or grow randomly every time you go to sleep.

180. "I had no choice but to shave my head."

181. "The best day of my life started with a freak hail storm."

182. "The worst day of my life began with a visit from my favorite person."

183. Write a story about a character that wakes up with a

tail.

184. Angels begin appearing all around the world.

185. Write about your ideal vacation.

186. Write a breakup scene from the point of view of the fish in the aquarium.

187. You are a waitress and your ex gets seated in your section.

188. You can be young and healthy forever but once a decade you would have to kill someone.

189. Write a scene or story that includes a purple coat, a

broken window and a singer.

190. Write an interview between you and your favorite literary character.

191. Write your own obituary.

192. Write your epitaph.

193. Write a six word story about your life.

194. You belong to the fashion police and you are on the biggest bust of your career.

195. You are invisible for 24 hours.

196. You find yourself sucked into the television set.

197. You find yourself sucked

into a board game.

198. Write a scene where your protagonist is trapped in a car.

199. Describe an eggplant without using the word purple.

200. Write a breakup scene between two best friends.

201. The devil has asked to buy your soul. Describe the bargain.

202. Your protagonist's house is haunted by a ghost. Who is it? Why are they there?

203. Write a showdown between two adversaries from the style of an old western but do not use any guns.

204. If the answer to the great question of life is 42, what is the question? Write a scene either describing the question or characters arguing over it.

205. Write a scene about a

person for whom everything they eat tastes like chicken.

206. A character has a visit from the mother that abandoned them years before.

207. Write about your dream job.

208. Your protagonist's favorite candy is being discontinued. They hatch a plan to murder the company president to stop them. Write the scene where they are trying to convince their friends to help.

209. You are hit by lightning and develop the ability to control

paper.

210. You accidentally insult a local god on your vacation. Suddenly you find yourself being chased by . . .

211. Write a scene about someone who is allergic to the sun and uses it to impersonate a vampire to join the local pride.

212. Write about the first time someone you know died.

213. The local high school reunion is affected by a truth spell. Everyone can only tell the full truth about their lives.

214. The local church is

affected by a lying spell. People can not tell the truth.

215. A large boulder rolls down and blocks the front door of house built into a hill trapping together two recently broken up former lovers.

216. Write a happy childhood memory.

217. Write about your last vacation.

218. Your character must choose between being smarter or better looking but which ever they choose, the opposite will happen to the other feature. They can be

smarter and uglier or prettier and dumber.

219. A squirrel starts stalking you.

220. Your protagonist develops the ability to communicate with light posts. They know he can understand them and will not stop talking.

221. Every morning your character must walk to the end of their driveway and fight the mailbox to prevent it from eating their mail and attacking the house.

222. A dozen strangers have

come to live with you as part of war cutbacks.

223. Your true love is marrying your brother. You have one last chance to try to stop it. What do you do?

224. Your character has the ability to change their race at will. What do they do with this power?

225. Every Thursday your character goes blind for 24 hours. At the same time, their partner goes deaf.

226. Your character speaks fluent baby.

227. Every day your character loses one of their senses. The next day it will be restored and a different sense will be lost.

228. You are turned back into your ten-year-old self.

229. Your character is a human being raised by an eagle and a lion that share custody.

230. Your character is allergic to the color orange. What happens to them when they see it? How does this affect their lives?

231. Your character is in charge of a new support group for people who over use "like" and

"umm".

232. It is your first day of assassin school and you have screwed up big time.

233. A souvenir brought home from a recent cruise mutates.

234. Write a letter to your past self warning you of your upcoming death.

235. Your apple orchard has become home to a vampire.

236. Write about a day when you were truly happy.

237. Write about the worst thing that every happened to you.

238. Write the author's

biography of the first stranger you see.

239. You find a mermaid in your swimming pool.

240. Your new neighbor is running a farm for old dogs to retire.

241. Close your eyes and turn around. Write a scene that starts with the first object you see when you open your eyes.

242. You develop the ability to fly but only while you are singing.

243. Your character is being stalked by a cloud.

244. Write the elevator pitch for your favorite book.

245. Write a scene where a cow and a horse both enter a single lane bridge from opposite sides and meet in the middle.

246. Describe the ugliest person in the world.

247. Describe the most beautiful person you can imagine.

248. Write a scene where the ugliest person and the most beautiful person in the world meet for the first time.

249. Describe what you are wearing with out using any of the

obvious color words. For example, no red but maroon is fine.

250. Describe your perfect day.

251. Write a synopsis of your first best selling novel (as long as you have not written it yet).

252. Your new boss is an absolute jerk. You have free license to do anything you want to him for 24 hours and he will never find out who did it. What do you do?

253. You are a cat. Describe your day.

254. Your couch has the ability to speak. How does this change your relationship?

255. You get turned into a dining room table for a day as

punishment for insulting a local deity.

255. There is a tree growing outside your window. Describe it.

256. Your new motto involves the words squirrel and honor. Write it.

257. There is a giant wall that entirely surrounds your town. Write about how this affects your life.

258. A man falls at your feet and utters the words, "It is done."

259. You are pitching your idea for a new kind of potato chip

flavor.

260. Write about the person who most influences your life.

261. You have the ability to see three minutes into the future. What do you do with this? How does it help or hinder you?

262. To you, everyone you see looks exactly like you.

263. The sun does not set at the end of the day. Why?

264. You are the child of a walrus and a human. Describe your typical day.

265. Your day is completely ruined when you forget to bring a

paper clip. How?

266. You are trying to sneak across the border. Where and why?

267. A young man stands on the edge of his balcony and takes one step.

268. Santa has sent you a warning letter that you are dangerously close to making the naughty list.

269. Write a scene entirely in the past tense about the day you married either your childhood sweetheart, a famous rock star or a former priest.

270. You desperately need to

complete something before your husband or wife comes home. What?

271. Every time you step on a crack you get a shooting pain up the left side of your body.

272. There is a nest of birds incubating their eggs in your hair or beard.

273. Everything you eat smells like nachos.

274. How would your life change if you could never sit down?

275. A dish and a spoon is all that is left of your childhood home.

276. You disappeared twenty years ago. Why? Where did you go? Why are you back now?

277. You are starting a fan convention honoring what?

278. "Tear through the car until you find it." Write a scene that starts with this sentence.

279. "What are you not telling us?" Write the next part.

280. You are invited to attend a long awaited lecture on string theory but it overlaps with your skydiving lessons.

281. Your teacher has accused you of cheating. Did you do it? If

so, how? If not, why do they think so?

282. It is late so you switch yourself to standby mode.

283. You lose a bet and must shave a design into your hair. Write about either the bet or the hair style.

284. Describe the outside of the closest building you can see using as many adjectives and adverbs as you can.

285. You come home from vacation to find an unexpected addition to your suitcase.

286. Write a scene that uses

at least three of the following words: elephant, sunscreen, toggle, battery pack and torture.

287. Describe how to cook an egg.

288. Write a scene where you tell your husband that he is not the father of your child.

289. Write a scene where you tell your pregnant girlfriend that you will not marry her.

290. Write a scene where three characters are all having dinner together. Each one has a secret that they don't want the rest to know.

291. You are standing outside a closed store when the zombies attack.

292. You wake up in bed with a strange woman and a piece of fruit.

293. Explain to a child where babies come from without using storks or sex in your explanation.

294. You are a father and you just burst in on your baby girl with a boy.

295. What do coins, windows and trees have in common?

296. Describe the perfect picnic.

297. A lion, a board game and a shopping mall.

298. Explain to your family why you named your son Cornelius.

299. "The punch landed squarely on my nose."

300. Write a scene that ends with, "which is why I will never again have an acrobat as a roommate."

301. This was the knot in my life.

302. You feel a breath upon your neck.

303. Is he ever on time?

304. Go for a walk and when you get back describe as many details as you can remember.

305. Describe yourself from God's point of view.

306. Describe yourself from the devil's point of view.

307. Describe yourself from an ant's point of view.

308. Write about your birth.

309. Write about death.

310. The voices in my head insist I am not going crazy.

311. Write dialog that is nothing but questions.

312. There are eyes in the window.

313. Describe something mundane from the point of view of a man who just suffered a terrible lose without ever revealing the man or his lose.

314. Describe something mundane from the point of view of a woman who is happily engaged.

315. You run into the one that got away.

316. I wish I could trust you but . . .

317. Write an explanation of why you didn't write yesterday.

318. Write a classified ad for a dragon for sale.

319. Write a scene where you swear you are telling the truth about what happened while clearly lying or exaggerating.

320. "I admit that I . . ."

321. Write a scene that ends with a big event such as a family reunion or a tornado.

322. Where the moonlight hit his skin, it began to smoke and

burn.

323. My husband doesn't hear me anymore.

324. "The sun never sets without . . ."

325. Write about a work of art.

326. When ever I _____, I feel as though _____. (Insert whatever comes to mind.)

327. I felt the needle prick my fingertip.

328. Who was the greatest fictional villain of all time? Why?

329. "For an entire year,

every morning found him . . ."

330. As soon as I killed him, I wished I could take it back.

331. "You shouldn't be here."

332. Object to a wedding.

333. "Every scar tells a story. This one . . ."

334. "It was her legs that did it."

335. "Elvis Presley never loved me."

336. "Smoking is required. Drinking is discouraged."

337. "I never drink before two AM."

338. Describe why your

favorite book should be required reading.

339. George was proud of his beard.

340. Elephants have a lot in common with astronauts.

341. You wake up two years in the future.

342. You hear a strange buzzing noise that is growing ever louder.

343. Your eyebrows keep growing.

344. You are invited to speak at an awards ceremony.

345. Write a scene involving

Popsicles, toilet paper and squirrels.

346. It hurt to remove the ring.

347. Having a third arm turned out to be very useful.

348. Write about losing a limb.

349. You join a band.

350. Your son inherits one trait from you. What is it?

351. I could never tell her and now she is gone.

352. The smell of his cologne brought back memories of when . . .

353. The elephant knew he was destined to be an acrobat.

354. You are a day of the week. Pick which one and describe your life.

355. He was by far my weirdest client.

356. All I could see were her shoes but I saw all I needed to know her completely.

357. A scent carried on the breeze.

358. Describe a scene where a cat is stuck in a tree from the viewpoint of either the cat or the tree.

359. You tell yourself you are going to be okay.

360. You are in a contest that you need to lose. Why? What kind of contest is it? What is at stake?

361. Write a letter to the court to prove that you are human.

362. You are inches away from the finish line when you stop.

363. Your girlfriend or boyfriend comes home with a haircut that you absolutely hate.

364. There is no evidence that Humpty Dumpty was an egg. What else could he have been?

365. A car, a motorcycle and a bicycle get into a fight as to which one is the best mode of transportation.

If you get stuck, try changing things up. If you usually type, then hand write. If you normally hand write, then try typing. If you normally write inside, try going outside or to another location. Try writing alone vs in public.

Set up a time every day to write even if it is only fifteen minutes. They say John Grisham wrote his first book one page a day before heading off to work. The best way to write is to be inspired but the best way for inspiration to find you is sitting down every day and writing.

Don't censor yourself as you write. If you let your inner critic tell you that some one is going to hate it, it just stifles you. Write what comes to mind. Write what you want to write. Worry about editing or whether to share it later. Now, just write.

Please consider reviewing this book. For a small author, reviews are the best way to get our books noticed.
Thank you,
EJ Divitt

Facebook: www.facebook.com/divittej

Twitter: @EJDivitt

Other books by EJ Divitt:

Etiquette As I Learned It

Have you ever found yourself at a loss as to what to say to someone at a funeral? Been overwhelmed at the thought of writing a thank you card? You have good intentions but just need a little help? This book is for you.

This is a guide to etiquette in every day situations and special occasions including weddings, funerals and thank you cards. It includes an all new etiquette quiz with answers at the back of the book.

I'm Engaged! Now What?

You're engaged! Congratulations! Now what do you do? Do you know where to begin the things you need to plan? What decisions you need to make?

You want your wedding to be amazing. "I'm Engaged! Now What?" will help you be your own wedding planner and make your dream day come true. It's all a matter of planning and preparation. In these pages, you will find what needs to be done and when it needs to be done. It takes the guess work out of planning your perfect day and sets you on the path to wedding planning bliss.

This edition also includes suggested <u>planning and budgeting checklists</u> as well as a list of important conversations to have with your fiance before you get married. Order now and start reading instantly.

Things Every Goddess Should Know . . . And We Are All Goddesses

Want your inner goddess to show? These are the things you need to know.
Have you ever read Greek mythology? Athena, Artemis and Aphrodite were incredibly powerful, beautiful and often petty and mistake prone. They were still goddesses.
Being a woman means you have the potential to be a force of nature. You are strong and beautiful in ways you have not yet begun to understand. You are a goddess in training. Things Every Goddess Should Know is full of life lessons, tips, hints and practical advice. Topics include:
Self Improvement and Self Help, Love and Sex, Relationships, Home and Garden, Health and Fitness, Safety and Security, Business, Money and Finances and The Practical

30 Second Etiquette

A series of quick essays on a variety of etiquette topics. Are you worried about how to behave at a wake? Is it okay to decline an invitation without giving a reason? How do you handle it when things get awkward? You'll recognize some things that have irritated you in others and see topics you have not considered. Covers over 35 topics of everyday etiquette situations.

The 30 Second Goddess

A Part of the "Things Every Goddess Should Know" series.

A collection of short lessons and thoughts on a variety of subjects. Includes lessons on starting a fire, figuring out your net worth, learning to appreciate yourself and even surviving the zombie apocalypse. How do you handle a frozen pipe? Need advice on debt management, tax brackets and budgeting?

Look inside before you buy and see the list of 35 topics covered.

Ever wondered about solar panels or if acts of God are covered by your home insurance?

EJ's Blogs:

"The Etiquette As I Learned It" blog

http://etiquetteasilearnedit.blogspot.com/

"The Things Every Goddess Should Know" blog

http://thingseverygoddess.blogspot.com/

Printed in Great Britain
by Amazon